Consolation No. 8

By. Dubiell, A, De Zarraga Lago.

Consolation No. 8

My Works:

Study No. 1

Study No. 2

Study No. 3

Study No. 4

Study No. 5

Study No. 6

Study No. 7

Study No. 8

Study No. 9

Study No. 10

Consolation No. 1

Consolation No. 2

Consolation No. 3

Consolation No. 4

Consolation No. 5

Consolation No. 6

Consolation No. 7

Consolation No. 8

Rapsodia a la Luna (Score) (All Instruments)

Rapsodia Alabaresque (score) (All Instruments)

String Concerto (Score All Parts)

Coming Soon:

Piano Concerto No. 1
(Two Piano)

Piano Concerto No. 1
(Score)

Piano Concerto No. 1
(All Parts)

Study No. 11

Study No. 12

Consolation No. 9

Consolation No. 10

Symphony No. 1
(Score & Parts)

String Concerto No. 2
(Score & Parts)

http://stores.lulu.com/notation
www.dubielldezarraga@yahoo.com

978-0-557-24355-6
2009 Dubiell A De Zarraga Lago

Consolation No.8

De Zarraga Lago, Dubiell, A.

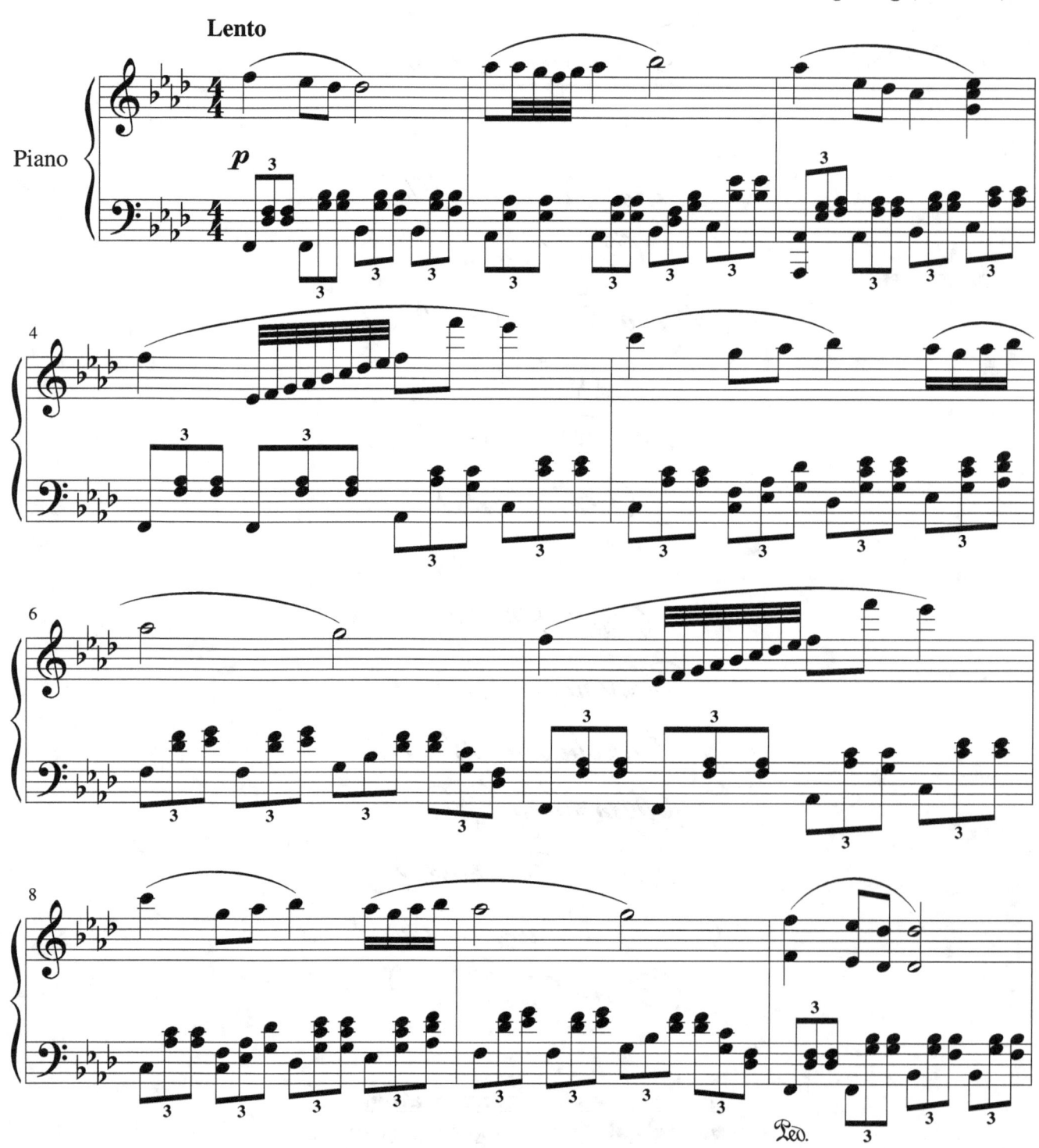

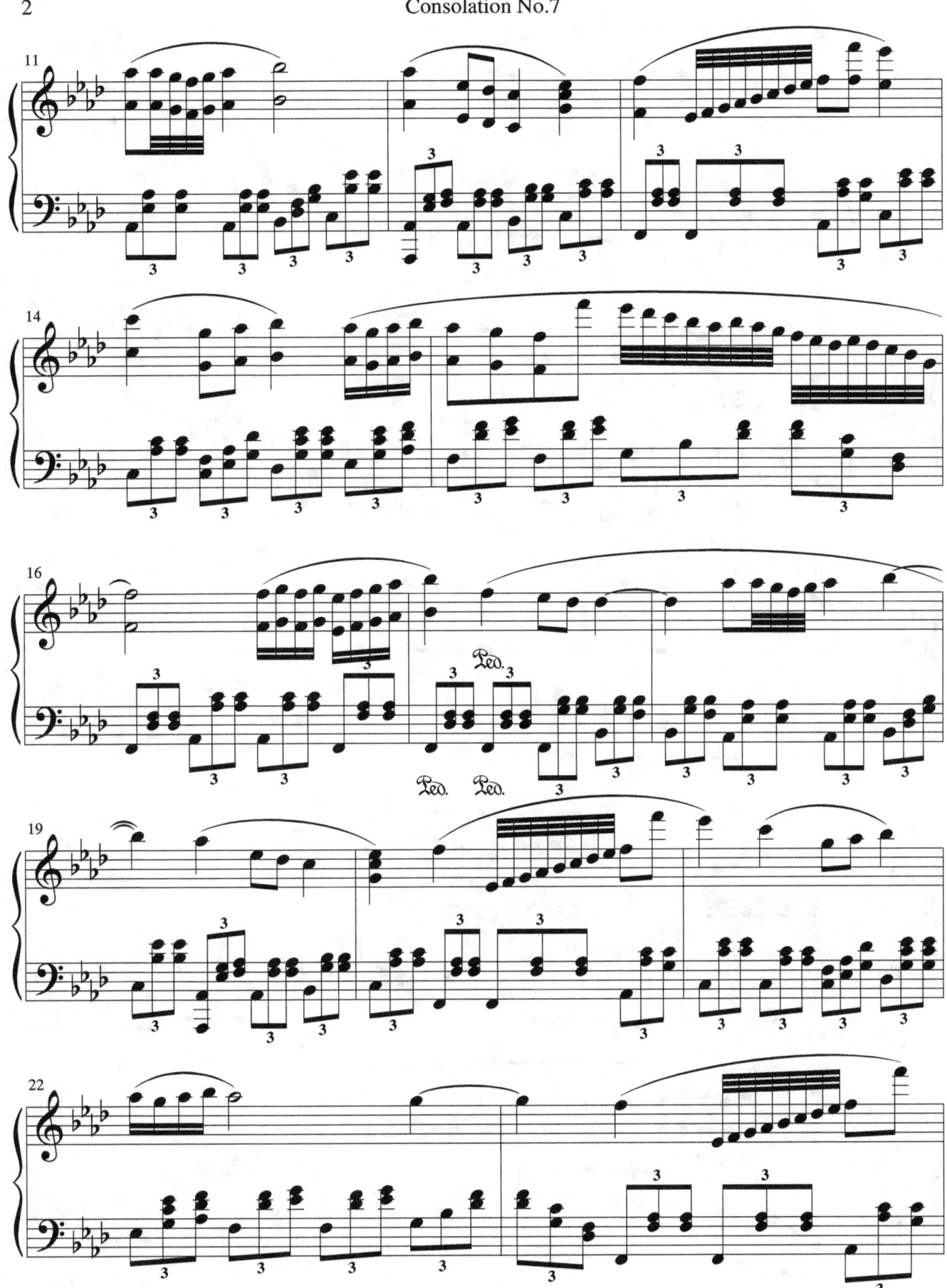

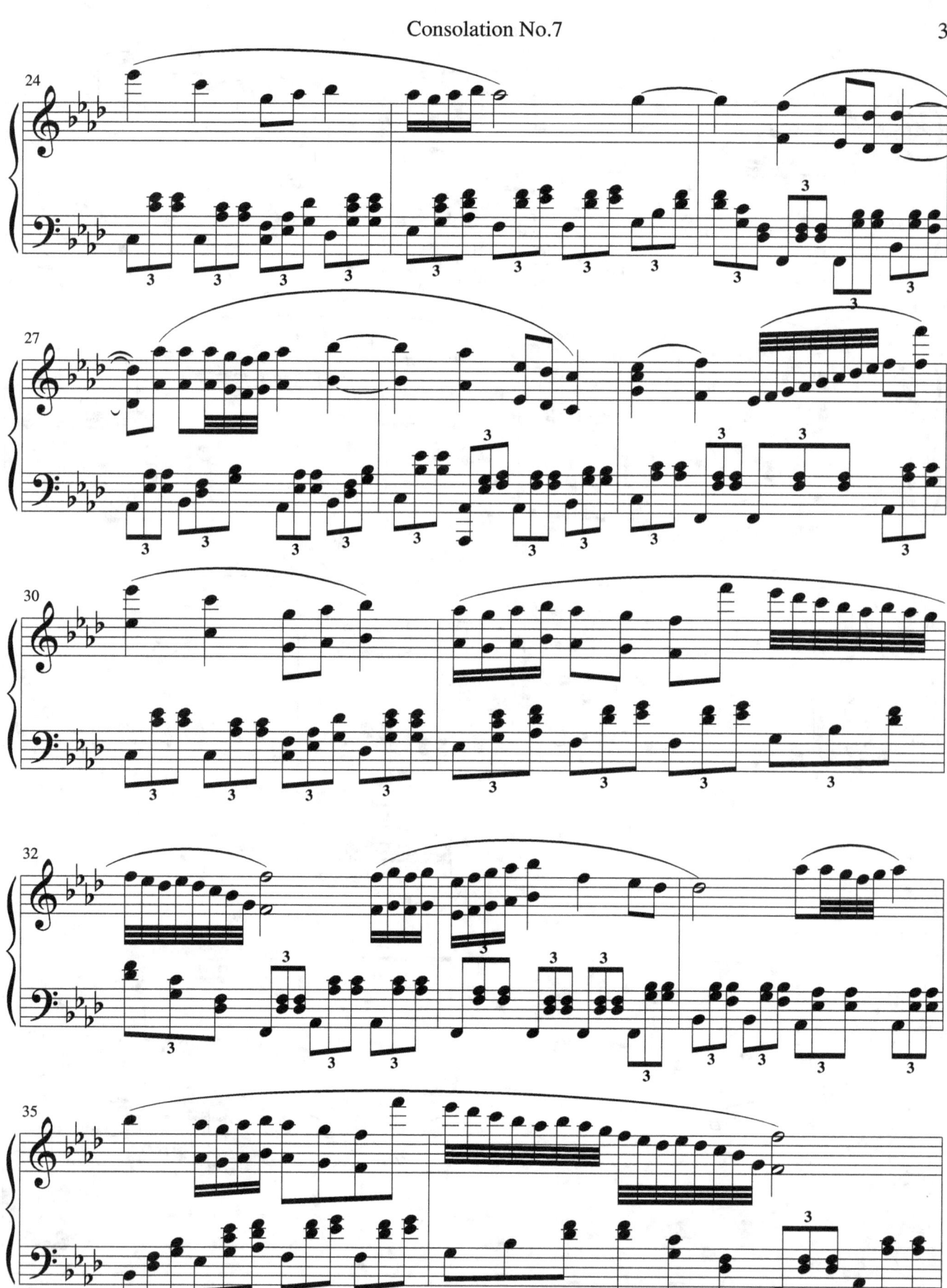

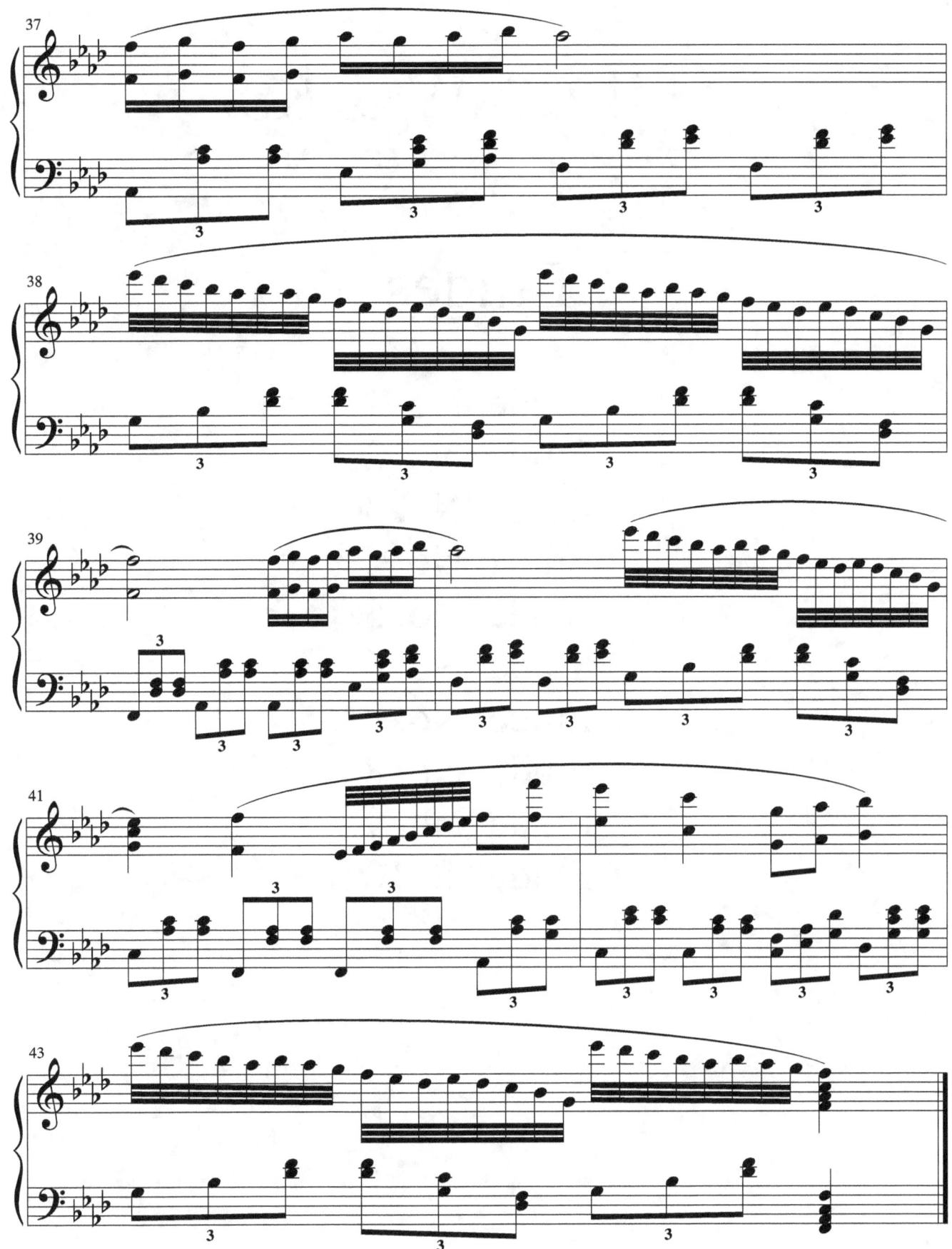

Other Works

Etudes

Etude No. 1
Etude No. 2
Etude No. 3
Etude No. 4
Etude No. 5
Etude No. 6
Etude No. 7
Etude No. 8
Etude No. 9
Etude No.10

Consolations

Consolation No.1
Consolation No.2
Consolation No.3
Consolation No.4
Consolation No.5
Consolation No.6
Consolation No.7
Consolation No.8
Consolation No.9
Consolation No.10
Consolation No.11
Consolation No.12
Consolation No.13

Rhapsodies

Rhapsody to the Moon
Rhapsody Alabaresque
Rhapsody in C Major

Concertos

Flute Concerto No.1
String Concerto No.1
String Concerto No.2
String Concerto No.3
Piano Concerto No.1

Preludes

www.lulu.com/dubiell

www.dezarragadubiell@yahoo.com

Notes

_____

_____

_____

_____

_____

_____

_____

_____

_____

_____

/

/

www.ingramcontent.com/pod-product-compliance
Lightning Source LLC
Chambersburg PA
CBHW081314180526
45170CB00007B/2704